I0786181

CHALLENGES OF IDENTITY

A PSYCHOLOGICAL PERSPECTIVE

CAROLINE NAMUGABI

CONTENTS

ACKNOWLEDGEMENTS

I am very grateful to all my mentors Mr. Jack Alecho-oita, Mr. William Nkata; let me close this emotional opening remark by saying, 'they were quite many'. At this point I should mention generally that am humbled by all the support that you all have offered during the making and the researching of this book, through numerous formal and informal discussions, practical advice, and insightful comments on the first draft.

I also must gratefully acknowledge my dear friend Mr. Nicholas Cooper, for the late-night discussions and contributions on the chapter of cultural identity whilst I was in the Netherlands, and in the United Kingdom.

I would also like to acknowledge many friends and colleagues from the field of psychology for their indirect contributions, friendly discussions, correspondence, and support that I immensely benefited from.

I now, most importantly, would like to acknowledge and give credit to my dearest mother Margaret, for giving me such great insight about my culture and cultural identity. Mum, am grateful to you for the continued and unstinting support whatever the challenging circumstances; and mentoring, more than anything else. Your ability to nurse, nurture and raise me and my other offspring without giving up says it all. To top all that is the cultural values you instilled in us all, and which unintended outcome is this book.

I love you Mum.

Dear READER

As you read this book, I ask that you read with an open mind and seek to learn and unpack more on the topic as you explore, learning continues.

I have done the talking to you now. I implore you from here on to raise both your cultural intelligence and capabilities so that you can live as well as you can with the challenges of identity.

Regards

Caroline Namugabi

Keys

In-group -   (us)

Out-group -   them (the group we don't belong to)

Groupthink -   Attempt and desire for harmony or conformity
               in a group

Introduction

Is Identity a Challenge?

The answer is yes, identity encompasses within it a lot of components both intrinsically and extrinsically; however, the challenges of identity only apply to beings that have a spirit or senses intact, this does not apply to objects.

In this book, Identity has been related to human beings within different environments and personal relations of the self and others dealing with the subject of identity. People to date, time after time are put in situations from birth where they must mold or face challenges of identity, weather these challenges develop their identity or not still the challenge remains one must address the self and identify the self. The question of WHO AM I, WHAT AM I.

In this book Chapter One, aims to unpack the definition of identity and how one can define identity in its' simplicity. Chapter Two deals the Social Identity, how one sees the self and their identity from a social view and how they relate that identity whilst in the social environment. Chapter Three, opens by exploring Cultural Identity, looking at identity from a cultural view and how culture can contribute to identity. Chapter Four, explores Identifying the Self, within Relationships, Attachments and The Actual Self, both externally and internally.

Chapter Five, is the Authors' Conner, where the author expresses her own experiences with identity and the challenges they've faced with identity. The theme of this book aims to look at Identity from a Psychological Perspective, with an intention to help the reader to understand and ascertain the causes and effects of challenges of identity. This can be seen or expressed though, Labeling, Behavior, Emotions, Expectations, Environments and Institutional Limitations; towards the nature of human beings within their natural state, which is freedom, from boxes of confinement both on Earth and Within Self.

CHAPTER

ONE

Identity defined

The subject of identity has been researched and studied over the years to date. To define it varies on the individual's perspective; the intent of this book is to take you through a process of a Psychological and Social perspective of identity. Identity can be defined as WHO or WHAT referring to a SUBJECT or an OBJECT. The challenge is exploring and seeking to find what these two components of subject and object are, within the biological make up or the environmental make up.

A SUBJECT (referring to a person) can change over time according to the surrounding factors around it. Identifying a SUBJECT is dependent on WHO? For example, biological make up of a person's DNA bloodline of what they are African or European, then culture which express the norms or practices (life style, food, systems) of their heritage, bloodline. The WHAT in this regard refers to two or three or more things referring to one subject, for example who you are (a subject, a person) within the person. There is also subordinate WHO's that can shape the subject towards two or three more components; for example, mother, father, daughter, son, teacher, artist.

As we have unpacked so far, that the SUBJECT identity, changes according to different factors. Whereas, on the other hand the OBJECT, stays the same, for example chair, house, school and so on. In this regard, it's not the WHO it's the WHAT that defines the OBJECT this is what gives the identity to the object. As noted by V, Vignoles et al Pg 2 Identity comprises not only:

> *"…who you think you are individually or collectively…"*

but also who you act as being:

"…In interpersonal and inter-group interactions and social recognition or how these actions are received from others, individuals, and groups…"

In popular and academic discourses, the term identity is sometimes applied as a catch all label for biological characteristics, psychological dispositions and/or socio-demographic positions, V, Vignoles et al Pg2.

As noted before we must first define the WHO and the WHAT first when dealing with the notion of identity, then deal with the characteristic attributes that unfolds with identity whilst dealing with the remaining factors. Research notes that, having a British passport does not automatically give someone a British identity, nor does having a skin colour. Therefore, this indicates that, there is more to identity then colour and holding a passport. According to individual's perspective regarding the WHO and the WHAT/SUBJECT or OBJECT. In support, academics note that, Identities are conceptually more complex than they may at first appear. From one point of view, they define who somebody is in terms of a trait, which might be anything from, for instance, a physical feature of the body, a belief, a genealogy, or a cultural preference. In effect they identify by placing individuals into groups who share that trait. And this has a consequence: implying that identity is won at the price of reducing individuality. My identity as a woman, for instance, both defines me and lumps me with, roughly, 50 per cent of the population, radically reducing my particularity. Furthermore the traits chosen to ascribe identity to an individual are always conditioned by something else, since whatever trait is chosen to fix identity, another one could have been chosen, even if it seems natural to identify people by, for instance, their gender (and it seems as if all known societies do in fact identify people by gender). Identities, then, are not given in terms of what individuals are, as a whole, but in terms of more or less arbitrarily selected features that they possess. For the most part, individuals have little power to choose what physical features will be used to identify them these are determined socially, from the outside[1].

CHANGES WITHIN IDENTITY

As pointed out before briefly above, identity is always evolving in relation to the subject and environmental changes. Processes of change take on different components and factors. This can be subjectively or objectively imposed, within environmental and circumstantial situations. Let me suggest here that the subject has an introvert character however later in life the subject acquires an extrovert character whereby he or she picks up criminal-like tendencies and later he or she gets the label "Criminal". These changes could be due the environment where the identity has been expressed or exposed too; for example, this could be due to experiences of war surroundings or peer pressure. One can refer to this as changes within identity, whereby one has acquired or developed a permanent or temporal identity of a criminal within this process.

---

[1] During Simon (2005) 'Debating Identity', in Cultural Studies: a critical introduction. London: Routledge, pp. 145-152

PSYCHOLOGICAL PERSPECTIVE I

Studies in psychology, according to Erickson et al[2], indicate that because subjects are social animals therefore social developments occurs relative to a person's interactions and transactions with the social environment. Subsequently here, the key factor is how does changes within identity affect identity; from a psychological perspective, questions such as how these criminal like tendencies where acquired would be in question. It is the acquirement of something that can bring about the process of change, as noted before social development occurs relative to a person's interactions and transactions with the social.

In this regard we can suggest that, the subject 'he' or 'she' may have acquired these criminal like tendencies because of "he" or "she's" social environmental influences or social interactions. These acquired tendencies can be influenced or caused by many factors such as biological impairments that can affect cognitive ability, for example, disabilities, improper conditioning, inappropriate learning, absence of appropriate role models.

Freud[3], too explains that, all humans have natural drives and urges that are repressed in the unconscious. Subjectively all humans can be regarded as having criminal tendencies these tendencies are curbed though the process of socialization values and culture, however, this does not account for cognitive process of the subject.

---

[2] Erikson, 1963 et al noted in Gross, PG 277, 2013.

[3] S (196) The ego and the id. In J Strachey (Ed). The Standard Edition of the Complete Works of Sigmund Freud (Vol 19, pp 12-66) London: Horgath Press. (Original work published 1923)

Smith and Bond et al[4] too notes that many psychologically useful cues are immediately apparent when interacting with others. Gender, age, race, physical attractiveness, body shape, baby-fadedness and so forth are all visually apparent. When the other talks, speech volume, speed, fluency and accentedness are likewise quickly available in addition to the content of the other's speech. Additional non-verbal behaviors, such as clothing, proxemics, body odour, posture, kinesic and patterns of gazing, can also be monitored. Each of these characteristics in others is informative about their personality, categorical cues, such as gender, provide information about the other though the mediation of stereotypes. It can be said that, because someone forms a cue about an individual's identity this does not mean that the individuals self-identity is exposed fully, therefore at this point this cue as we can see only accounts for the immediate encounter with that individual. Therefore, note that when looking at a subject one must evaluate all aspect of this identity which maybe dependent on differential and unfolding situations.

Changes within identity can be very fluid according to the process of change via different factors as discussed above. This could also include age, developmental growth, environment and so on; therefore, here the key factor is how does changes affect identity. For explanation, lets suggest a John is transsexual who has an identity already of a male, however a John prefers to be a Mary. This implies that, a John must transform within a new identity as a woman not as a man. Here, there would be some changes within his identity such as attitude, dress code, maybe

---

[4] 1998 Pg 235 [See full in Reference]

social networks, tone of speech, name, etc., that a John may have to change. Taken to the extremes, maybe a body change transformation surgery and so forth. These are some of the changes within identity, a John's character may not change but his identity and attitude or behavioral traits are subjected to change in line with the new identity.

PSYCHOLOGICAL PERSPECTIVE ii

How does this affect old and the new identity, emotionally, psychologically such as a John, was affected by the identity of male, because emotionally a John did not hold or experience emotional traits of a male. A John identified more with the feminine attributes such as, emotional, very domesticated nurturing, irrational. How does this transition affect the subject? Usually subjects experience sense of not belonging this can cause depression, stress anxiety and form addictions. As a result of these changes within identity, subjects can or may face, stigmatization and discrimination oftentimes, lethal violence and denial of basic human rights.

In support, During Simon[5] quoted in Salih 2010, Fuss 1995 [6] express that;

> *'...The fit between an identity and an individual self, is therefore, structurally loose, and is often thought of as requiring processes of identification in order to be sealed...'*

---

[5] (2005), Simon During: Cultural Studies, A critical Introduction. New York: Routledge 2005 pp. 145-152

[6] (2010) Sara Salih: Representing Mixed Race in Jamaica and England from the Abolition Era to the present, 2010: Routledge research in Postcolonial literature.

Certainly, individuals differ as to the degree of intensity with which they connect to identities. Indeed, significant numbers of people struggle to dis-identify from detaching themselves from given identities. In the case of transsexuals the most famous of such groups. (In this case we have an identity based on dis-identification since, according to the cultural logic of gender-identities, an individual born a man can never wholly become a woman.) And where identities have a low cultural value, individuals ascribed such identities can internalize negative images of themselves. In such cases, the process of identification can cause psychic damage.

SELF PRESENTATION

After these changes occur, whether during childhood or adulthood one then oftentimes self-identify themselves. Where they feel they belong, this oftentimes happens during different process of life stages according to Age, Ethnic identity and Culture.

People present themselves differently in social groups and environments, there is often some influence in this according to the social environment or environment one is in. For example, according to some African cultures, such as Uganda (to name a few), professional people drop their professional hats when socializing in different social environments of entertainment, for example, clubs, parties etc. It's reported that if a Doctor goes to a club or a party he or she may still carry themselves as a Doctor or Lawyer and so on. Moreover, the people, if known to them, will also seek to still identify them with what their professional role is regardless of the environments there are in.

Whereas in Europe, professionals present themselves according to their social environment, and not by the achievements they have acquired. A doctor or a lawyer becomes a normal person outside his or her profession. In support academics, such as in Goffman, noted in Newman et al 1958, report[7] to quote:

"…Significant portion of social life is influenced by the images we form of others. We typically form impressions of people based on an initial assessment of their social group membership, their personal attributes (for example physical attractiveness) and the verbal and nonverbal messages they provide. Such assessments are usually accompanied by set of expectations we've learned to associate with members of certain social groups or people with certain attributes. Such, judgments allow us to place people in broad categories and provide a degree of predictability in interactions"[8]…"

PSYCHOLOGICAL PERSPECTIVE

Self-Presentational Strategies

o Negotiating an identity is an important goal that we pursue throughout us

o From childhood on, we develop increasingly effective strategies for

o presenting ourselves to others (Aloise Young[9], 1993). Table 5.5 lists five important self-presentational strategies: ingratiation, self -promotion, intimidation, exemplification,

---

[7] Sociology exploring the architecture of everyday life: David, M, Newman et al 1958, Pg 109, published 1958.

[8] Sociology exploring the architecture of everyday life: David, M, Newman et al 1958 published 1958.

[9] Cited in Lord, C, G, Published 1997, *Social Psychology*, Publisher Christopher P, Klein. Pg 191-192, 1997

and supplication (Jones & Pittman[10] 1982).

Each of the five strategies pursues a different emotion, involves a different set of actions, and risks a different unwanted result. Ingratiation is the most frequently used of the five self-presentational strategies. The goal is to be liked. Almost everyone finds it rewarding to be liked by other people. As a result, as noted by Lord C. G[11], people usually put their best foot forward especially in job interviews and similar situations by modestly showing their likable traits and by complimenting other people or doing favors for them.

As we have explored in this chapter, in conclusion, 'Identity' can take a process of acquired labeling, biological process and cognitive abilities, most of these changes require environmental and social influences alongside parental influences. As we begin to unpack the subject of identity in this book, am in the hopes of neat picking the salient factors on the subject. 'Identity' is a big field of study which is still ongoing due to its changing residue as life and science progresses.

---

[10] As cited in Lord, C, G, Published 1997, *Social Psychology*, Publisher Christopher P, Klein. Pg 191-192, 1997

[11] Source Lord, C, G, Published 1997, *Social Psychology*, Publisher Christopher P, Klein. Pg 191-192, 1997.

CHAPTER

TWO

Social Identity

Research suggests that, social identity can be defined as the groups with which we associate ourselves with for example student, social clubs, etc. Within our social identity we tend to categories with these groups. For example, a student put into the school system even though they don't identify themselves as student you just know you need to be there and learn. Therefore this leads to social categorization, which then leads to social identification then you may start to identify yourself as a student, Social identity is a person's awareness or knowledge that he or she belongs to a social category and that the individual can identify with that social norm, can be seen in groups settings or private settings such as family gartering or gatherings; and can be seen or enacted out by two principles such as 'In group' or 'Out group' which simply refers to a group acceptance or non-acceptance from the group let's call it the IN or OUT of the circle.

Social identity theory as noted in Rogers Pg 244-24[12], proposes that people's individual psychological processes are transformed in group settings, people come to identify themselves with social groups and, thereby, to define themselves as having the characteristics of that social group. Therefore, the identity is set according to the settings of those social norms, however this

---

[12] (2003) Wendy Rogers: Social Psychology, Experimental and Critical Approaches: Published 2003, Philadelphia.

can be arguable as we explore. The requirement of these social settings may require different identity beliefs and identity acceptance. Subsequently, social groups search as, institutional, or organisational groups oftentimes form a social identity that enforces categorization on the individual whereby requirements such as staff conduct, or organisational rules must be followed.

In support, group studies such as J Hennessy,[13], and M West, found that, Employees in the organisation showed evaluative in-group favoritism by rating their own work group more positively than others. Second, they showed behavioral in-group favoritism by allocating more money to their own group than to others. Identification with work group was positively related to evaluative 'In-group' favoritism as predicted but was not related to discriminatory 'In-group' favoritism, organisational identification was negatively related to discrimination in favor of the 'In-group', the study provided some support for social identity theory, source [14].

This indicates, that if we are received positively with the groups we relate with then we can form a positive social identity within those environmental social norms. Therefore, for example our social identity or how we identify ourselves within that group or social surroundings depends on the acceptance of our 'In-group' Circle of that group. In relation to organisational groups, it can be alluded that one may negatively feel negative towards the organisation or institution that they work for due to

---

[13] Josephine Hennessy and Michael, A, West; First Published June 1, 1999. Research Article

[14] Intergroup Behavior in Organizations, A field Test of Social Identity Theory: Josephine Hennessy and Michael, A, West; First Published June 1, 1999. Research Article:

the social group within that organisation in that they may not have a social identity within the groups of the organisation.

Therefore, they may belong or can be identified as a member of the 'Out-group' circle, in addition, this individual maybe category as a loner within the organisation simply because they may not have an 'In-group' that they socially identify with. However, within other social environments this individual's social identity may be with the 'In-group' circle. In a similar vein, according to Turner (1982) to quote;

> *'…when people identify with their group, they undergo depersonalization they abandon some of their uniqueness and engage in a process of self-stereotyping…'*

Suggesting that, in order, to strengthen their identification as noted in Rogers 2003 Pg 245[15] to quote:

> *'…people are motivated to take on and define themselves in terms of stereotypical characteristic of the group…'*

PSYCHOLOGICAL PERSPECTIVE

Experimental social psychology views the self as molded by social processes (such as socialization and identification with social groups (and social influences such as the kind of upbringing a person is given).

For example, a young woman who has seen herself as heterosexual adopts a new style of clothes and demeanor when she identifies herself as lesbian; another would be a young

---

[15] (2003) Wendy Rogers: Social Psychology, Experimental and Critical Approaches: Published 2003, Philadelphia.

woman who was brought up as a non–religious adopts the veil and the devout demeanor when she identifies herself as a Muslim. In both cases the young women cease to see how to dress and how to behave as a matter of personal choice, but rather by reference to the group with which they identify. In a similar vein, Turner (1991) [16] indicates that, such self-stereotyping can be very fluid, and shift according to the reference group. For example, yet another woman may identify herself as belonging to a reference group of professional women at work, yet as a babe when she goes out socializing on a girlie night out and adjust her dress and demeanor accordingly, in each case as noted in Rogers, (2003) Pg245[17] these individual women are conforming to a stereotype.

Social identity theory therefore suggests that people gain their sense of identity via their association with social groups. When their 'in-group' does well, they can enjoy in its mirrored glory, when it does bad, this can weaken them. In this regard, Social Identity works differently according to different environments and surroundings alongside relational factors, cultural factors and so forth.

GROUP IDENTITY

When looking at the word group, one must first unpack what group is, the Business dictionary defines group as a collection of individuals who have regular contact and frequent interaction, mutual influence, common feeling of camaraderie, and who

---

[16] Ibid Turner quotes p 23
[17] Ibid 15.

work together to achieve a common set of goals, source[18]. Now as we alluded in Chapter One, identity is the WHO or WHAT referring to a SUBJECT or an OBJECT, by exploring and seeking to find what these two components of subject and object are, within the biological make up or the environmental make up. In reflection to these suggestions of group and identity, a group identity is how the group identify themselves within their interactions, such as social, environmental, or organisational. It's been suggested that norms of group interactions have been developing increasingly over the years. People seem to interact as a group more especially in organisational settings and for the most part social setting and religious gatherings.

Additionally, in reflection to group identities, During Simon (2005)[19], notes that, the terms by which identities are ascribed do not usually describe traits or groups neutrally. They are culturally inflected, and in the last instance are determined by power relations within a community, especially how these shape social relations between those using the identity-descriptor and those to whom the descriptor applies. Thus, for instance, it matters a great deal whether an American black person is called a nigger, an African American, a black, a Negro, etc. Each of these terms marks an identity which is both the same as (in that it marks out the same group) and different from (in that it has different connotations) each of the other terms. And each of these terms may change its meaning depending on who is using it, and in what context, the groups affirmatively use some

---

[18] Business Directory
[19] Ibid 5

identity words they describe (and thus they mark self-identities), others are not. Quite often, words used by others to define a group insultingly or prejudicially are appropriated by the group themselves and turned into a term marking self-identity, usually after passing through a brief phase where they are used ironically: hippie, punk, nigger itself, for instance.

Tajfel[20] reports that the groups (e.g. social class, family, football team etc.) that people belonged to can be an imperative source of pride and self-esteem. Groups, give us a sense of social identity a sense of belonging to the social world. It can be said that, to increase our self-image, we enhance the status of the group to which we belong. For example, Africa is the best country in the world! We can also increase our self-image by discriminating and holding prejudice views against the 'Out-group'. For example, the Americans, English etc., are a bunch of losers! By this view, we divided the world into "them" and "us" based through a process of social categorization (i.e. we put people into social groups). This is known as 'In-group' and 'Out-group'. Social identity theory claims that the 'In-group' will discriminate against the 'Out-group' to enhance their self-image.

As noted before, there are many group identities; in this chapter we going to aim to unpack one which is organisational group identity. Usually, when people are a part of an organisation, they tend to identify themselves within the groups of that organisation, this mostly occurs within big organisations such as hospitals, universities and so on. People feel a sense of

---

[20] Ibid Source: https://www.learning-theories.com/social-identity-theory-tajfel-turner.html

belonging for the most part if they are a part of a group. For example a group of nurses a group of doctors working together and forming their own identity within the organisation. However, research reports that, individuals could be part of a group within the same institution and still feel like outsiders, in that they may not have identified themselves with the norms or networks or the working mechanism of that group.

Studies such as Hennessy and A. West (1999)[21], also found that, employees in the organisation showed evaluative 'In-group' favouritism by rating their own work group more positively than others. They showed behavioural 'In-group' favouritism (discriminatory 'in-group' favouritism) by allocating more money to their own group than to others. The study also for that, 'Identification' with work group was positively related to evaluative 'in-group' favouritism as predicted, but was not related to discriminatory in-group favouritism. They found that, these results thus provide some support for social identity theory and, for the first time, demonstrate a relationship between work group identification and evaluative in-group favouritism (positive), and between organisational identification and discriminatory 'In-group' favouritism (negative), source[22]. Therefore, this indicates that being a part of the 'In-group' comes with more beneficial rewards when dealing with group identity as the group identify themselves being a part of the 'In-group' provides the individual with a relatable identity; therefore

---

[21] Josephine Hennessy and Michael, A, West; First Published June 1, 1999. Research Article

[22] Josephine Hennessy and Michael A. West: Small Group Research, Vol. 30 No. 3, June 1999 361-382

'In-group' discrimination occurs when an individual's identity is not relatable to that group. Group identity varies according to the social and environmental norms of the individual, how the individual identifies themselves within the group depends upon the group and the dynamics and requirements of that group. For example a church group, a sports group a think tank group a cultural group a student group and so on.

In addition, research notes that, when people are deeply involved in a close-knit group, their desire for unanimity can override their motivation to consider alternative courses of action13. Groupthink is not a new phenomenon. From the training of soldiers to act as a unitary squad to the behaviour of urban rioters, it has been known for a long time that people can conform to group norms to a startling extent. A group whose identity is based on winning and losing, for example members of a political party whose identity is linked to their performance in an election, can strongly activate a sense of 'In-group'/'Out group' that is an inherent part of human behaviour. From an evolutionary perspective it was essential to be part of a group to survive, modern neuroscience suggests we possess powerful mechanisms to encourage collective behaviour and avoid being rejected. When a person deviates from an opinion held by the wider group, the brain evaluates it as an error and consequently adjusts behaviour. The brain creates a strong incentive for 'toeing the line' through the reward centres of the brain and at the same time it experiences rejection from a group in a similar way to physical pain. As this is at a predominantly subconscious level, people are often unaware that they are altering their behaviour or being influenced by others, source[23].

CONFORMITY

Conformity, has been defined as a type of social influence involving a change in belief or behaviour to fit in with a group, source[24]. This can also be defined as *"yielding to group pressures"*, as noted by Crutchfield, (1955) noted in Rogers (2003)[25]. Group pressure may take different forms, such as bullying, persuasion, teasing, criticism, and so on, conformity is also known as majority influence. Studies such as Asch(1951), noted in Rogers (2003)[26] found that, people tend to conform whilst in a group, reporting that, during his experiment 25% of subjects in the experiment steadfastly continued to give their own independent judgement, despite the repeated pressure of six or seven other people all giving the same wrong response, was about 5%. However, on the other hand the remaining 70% of the subjects conformed some or most of the time. When Asch[27] asked subjects, who had conformed to report on their findings after the experiment, they said they felt very uncomfortable. The majority however said they knew they were seeing things differently from the other members of the group but felt increasingly uncertain about their own judgement. Others said they were right but went along with the group so as

---

[23] http://www.bps.org.uk/system/files/Public%20files/Comms-media/Making%20better%20decisions.pdf

[24] https://simplypsychology.org/conformity.html

[25] Ibid 12

[26] Ibid 12

[27] Ibid 24.

not to stand out. These conforming subjects as noted in Rogers[28] Pg 273 to quote:

> *'...they felt self-conscious, anxious, and even lonely, and feared disapproval...'*

I am also persuaded by Asch's (1951) noted by in Roger (2003)[29] research on conformity. Although his research was done in the 1950s this research may differ in contemporary times according to countries and social environments. For example, England is a country that is known to teach people to maintain a culture of exclusiveness whereas continents like Africa teaches inclusiveness, so therefore people within those social environments like Africa may have to conform to their cultural norms or group settings due to the countries customs. Cultures where collectivist values dominate tend to be more conforming than individualist cultures, and it can be said that, generally whilst in a group, people may conform or feel to conform toward the norms of the group or even work faster and better at a task due to a mere presence of others.

The Social Facilitation Theory [30] supported this whereby, Triplett 1898[31] who used it in his research on the speed records of cyclists, noticed that racing against each other rather than against the clock alone increased the cyclists' speeds. He attempted to duplicate this under laboratory conditions using children and fishing reels. There were two conditions: the child

---

[28] (2003) Wendy Rogers: Social Psychology, Experimental and Critical Approaches: Published 2003, Philadelphia.

[29] Ibid 24

[30] https://www.simplypsychology.org/Social-Facilitation.html

[31] https://www.simplypsychology.org/Social-Facilitation.html

alone and children in pairs but working alone. Their task was to wind-in each amount of fishing line. Triplett reports that many children worked faster in the presence of a partner doing the same task, source[32].

However, you may have one or two independent individuals with a consolidated identity that may not conform easily. It can be said that, people conform oftentimes for fear of disapproval. Oftentimes this can be due to a sense of the individual wanting to belong or seeking to belong within that environment or social surroundings. This can also be the unwritten social contract according to the environment and of course on the other hand one may have other issues to conform or not to conform, such as medical issues like mental health, to name a few.

How then can this effect the individual's identity? Conforming can affect the individual's identity both temporally or indefinitely. Whereby according to the influences that surround the individual identity can be shaped or influenced indefinitely or temporally due to conforming. For example, if an individual who has been incarcerated or confined in an environment for a long time, they can begin to conform to the conditions of those environments whereby it can shape a new identity for them, good or bad due to the conditioned or influenced setting. In addition to the above findings, when looking at conforming on a bias level; it has been found that, research within the psychological realm also found that Conformation bias People tend to look for, notice, and remember information that fits

---

[32] Ibid 14

with their pre-existing expectations and to ignore or dismiss contradictory information. Our understanding of the world is not objective – we see events and interpret information in a way that confirms our beliefs and seek out evidence that matches. It's been suggested that, Conformation bias can have a huge impact on the quality of decision-making across many professions. In medicine, when a doctor takes a patient's medical history they may ask questions to confirm their earlier judgement, rather than seeking evidence that will disprove their hypothesis. Consequently, they reach an early conclusion and can fail to unearth key information that could be critical to the patient's diagnosis, source [33].

In this chapter we have learned the different roles that people play when faced with social identity and within the different social norms of the social networks. It's understood that different components that contributes to individual's social identities such as Conformity, Groups, Social settings and social environmental settings, manifest in different ways and are influenced by different factors within that social situation. How the subject identifies himself within this these social setting will depend on the individuals' cognisant understanding of their social environment.

---

[33] http://www.bps.org.uk/system/files/Public%20files/Comms-media/Making%20better%20decisions.pdf

CHAPTER

THREE

Cultural Identity

To understand cultural identity, we need to first define what culture is; at its simplest form, culture is a system of practice that is accepted by a group. The word culture can mean to cultivate a school of thought based upon a particular cultural authenticity, self-worth and self-preservation are ways in which to build and guide from cultural ethics and motto. To understand cultural identity, we need to understand four differential factors, the individual's personal identity as it relates to social identity within a culture and the social systems that are dictated by that cultural identity.

Cultural identity refers to a culture, that the individual it relates too or can relate too. For example, the host culture of a country can be, England, however within England there are subordinate and distinct cultures such as Scottish, Irish, and Welsh that have identity and social systems to follow. These have been authenticated based upon a school of thought and self-preservation and cultural ethics that have been built overtime to guide the cultural identity of the Scottish, Irish and Welsh people whilst still retaining the host countries national culture. In addition, British, Afro-Caribbean and Africans tend to assimilate to the host countries national culture whilst retaining their original cultural identities. In this regard let's suggest some immigrant from an African background or heritage, immigrates to England maybe arising from war issues, human rights and so forth. During their time of settlement, they engage in the host countries customs.

It's been suggested that oftentimes depending on the age group immigrants must assimilate to the host countries culture, customs and can find it hard to settle in to the culture, however, the younger generation has been found to easily adapt and fit in.

Whilst engaging in to the host countries culture, immigrants whose culture and traditions are unfamiliar to mainstream groups tend to integrate into their own new social organisation and leadership structures, the older generation aim to retain their cultural identity, weather at home or by their social groups. In a similar vein, in order to preserve cultural identity research notes that, the Chinese and Asian culture place heavy emphasis on taking care of one's family. Therefore, indicating that, taking care of their family is a contribution to civic welfare, because healthy families lead to healthy society. In other words, family relationships form the basis for Chinese/Asian social organisation and behavior, they also maintain placing a high value on education by forming their own schools that teach in Chinese/Asian, which gives them the ability of retaining their cultural identity across generations weather at home or aboard these are the social systems that are used in the Chinese and Asian community.

Case Study

I am persuaded by Rosenthal and Feldman (1992) [34] who assessed each of these elements of identity among first and

---

[34] (1998, Pg 274) Peter B.Smith and Michael H.Bond: Social Psychology Across Cultures. Second Edition, Published 1998

second generation Chinese immigrants to Canada and Australia, in comparison with Chinese students in Hong Kong. As expected, they found only moderate linkage between their various measures of ethnic identity. Cultural practices and labeling oneself as Chinese declined in the first generation but fell no further in the second. Subjective evaluation of one's identity and importance attached to Chinese cultural practices did not decline at all. The authors conclude that behavioral aspects of cultural identity may change slowly over time, but as Smith and Bond, Pg 274[35] noted that the internal components are more resistant to change.

On the other hand, Afro Caribbean and African immigrants whilst aboard tend to use very different social systems to preserve cultural identity. It's been reported that they put on musical events such as festivals, concerts, church gatherings, beauty pageants, conventions and forums to name a few. It's been suggested that Afro Caribbean and Africans tend to easily assimilate to the host countries national culture whilst aboard compared to the Asian and the Chinese immigrants. In most African / Afro Caribbean communities it is common to find one or more churches that are the focal point for social, economic, and political activities, spirituality, especially Christianity, provides hope among African / Caribbean people, oftentimes they use the practice of church and spirituality as a part of their cultural identity.

Subsequently, these behaviors, norms, social systems, within the African /Caribbean have been known to have merged during

---

[35] Peter B.Smith and Michael H.Bond: Social Psychology Across Cultures. Second Edition, Published 1998.

the slavery of African people, music was the most used tool during slavery amongst African people.

It's also been documented, that African / Afro Caribbean people were taken away from their original home lands and where taken to European countries and the United States of America to be enslaved.

Other researches also note that due to these experiences many African/Afro Caribbean's to date are still experiencing some residues of psychological traumas within identifying who they are and their race alongside belonging.

PSYCHOLOGICAL PERSPECTIVE[36]

African-American to date alongside Afro-Caribbean's struggle with a multi-faceted conception of self, a double consciousness. They are constantly trying to reconcile the two cultures that compose their identity. Early African-Americans saw Africa as their homeland and the place they belonged while they saw America as the land they were brought to against their will to be enslaved. However, because of the experiences of slavery and acculturation, early African Americans ideas of both of their identities were greatly distorted. The American Plantation system created slave's populations that mixed Africans from different ethnic groups and discouraged African cultural practices in attempts to prevent slave revolts. As slaves, Africans were forbidden to speak their original languages, stripped of their original African names, converted to Christianity, discouraged from expressing themselves in

---

[36] Source: Double consciousness-Wikipedia

dancing, and not allowed to use drams. Such restrictions ensured the distortion of African cultural legacy and that the same legacy would be severely impaired, if not lost completely, among later generations of African Americans.

In addition to the slavery issue, one can look at this and understand the thought processes of assimilation amongst African's and Afro Caribbean people. These realities developed from the enforcement of slavery. And they seem to have been carried on amongst generations. Whereas, the Asian and the Chinese community just adapt to the environment they are in rather than assimilate. In this regard, oftentimes majority of Africans and Afro Caribbean to date may seem to battle cognitively with their cultural identity more whilst aboard than the Asian/Chinese; this brings about a double consciousness state; as stated in W.E.B DU Bois double consciousness, book The Souls of Black Folk 1903[37].

Unpacking the double consciousness briefly: a cultural identity view.

WEB DU Bois 1903 The Souls of Black Folk: notes that, double consciousness:

> *"...It is a peculiar sensation, this double consciousness, this sense of always looking at one's self through the eyes of others, of measuring one's soul by the tape of a world that looks on in amused contempt and pity. One ever feels his two-ness- an American, a Negro; two souls, two thoughts, two unreconciled strivings; two warring ideals in one dark body, whose dogged strength alone keeps it from being torn*

---

[37] W.E.B DU BOIS, The Souls Of Black Folk 1903, Pg 2, in The Dover Thrift Edition edited 1994.

asunder. The history of the American Negro is the history of this strife -this longing to attain self- conscious manhood, to merge his double self into a better and truer self. In this merging, he wishes neither of the older selves to be lost. He does not wish to Africanize America, for America has too much to teach the world and Africa. He wouldn't bleach his Negro blood in a flood of white Americanism, for he knows that Negro blood has a message for the world. He simply wishes to make it possible for a man to be both a Negro and American without being cursed and spit upon by his fellows, without having the doors of opportunity closed roughly in his face[38]..."

As one starts to unpack this notion of the double consciousness, we can see psychologically how the W.E.B DU BOIS, sentiments are still playing roles within contemporary times of today both in Europe and America. It's been reported that Black Africans are treated different within the social systems of both Europe and the USA. More so are reported to have the most percentages of prisoners within that race. On the other side according to the residue of what was carried over by the slavery trauma as mentioned above where men and women were made to stay apart and their cultural norms were forbidden. Other reports also indicate a high level of communication breakdown between black men and women alongside marriage break down within the black African race. Moreover, black women are oftentimes seen as insecure, bitches, bleaching their skin to become lighter/whiter rather than embracing their own skin colour as this is what is seen to

---

[38] Source: W.E.B DU BOIS, The Souls Of Black Folk 1903, Pg 2, in The Dover Thrift Edition edited 1994.

be marketed as beautiful on television/pictures and in society within Europe and American culture.

Considering all the above, therefore, where a double consciousness can be seen though societies impact on the Individual's personal outlook of him or herself, one can start to experience a double consciousness of their cultural identity depending upon their upbringing. Psychologically a double consciousness can cause emotional trauma such as, insecurity, anxiety, abandonment issues, mental health issues and so on. Cultural identity in this regard can be related to belonging whereby for example a subject who emigrated from Africa to Europe at a younger age, then returns to their native country in their maturity. During their return, they learn that, that sense of not belonging becomes assimilation as they are forced to learn some new customs. In this regard, the social systems of that culture are viewed different by the individual according to what they knew. This could be food, dressing, activities, etc., the subject could also be viewed as a European person by the African people due to his or her mannerism. This is where the double consciousness kicks in the idea of being faced with two cultural identities and yet not feeling that you fully belong to one or the other. Smith, and Bond, Pg 273[39], also note that the historical legacy of colonialism has left many people worried about the potential of inter-cultural contact for the destruction of native heritages. In extreme forms, there is genocide or ethnic cleansing: in other forms, there is assimilation, whereby a stronger cultural group absorbs the weaker, so that its distinctive organisation, rituals, dress, architecture, crafts and so

---

[39] Peter B.Smith and Michael H.Bond: Social Psychology Across Cultures. Second Edition, Published 1998

forth simply disappear. At the individual level, there are spirited concerns expressed about the loss of cultural identity which may arise out of inter/intra-cultural contact.

National culture and identity

The national culture of a country is usually used as the identity of that country. For example, if within the country there are a great number of people that form a main culture and this culture is practiced by a huge amount of people within the country this can be usually seen as the National culture. Therefore, giving that individual country the National identity via those practices, this usually entails cultural customs such as food, music, and language, to name a few.

National identity can be thought as a collective product, through socialization, a system of beliefs, values, assumptions, and expectations is conveyed to group members. The collective principles of national identity may include national symbols, traditions, and memories of national experiences and achievements. These collective fundamentals are rooted in the nation's history. Contingent on how much the individual is exposed to the socialization of that system; people incorporate national identity to their personal identity to different degrees and in different ways. The collective elements of national identity may become important parts of individual's definition of the self and how they view the world and their own place in it.

The identity of this national culture varies according to how it's maintained within that country, in that it may shift, according to the subcultures that are within the country. For example, in

England the Irish and Scottish cultures and social systems may become England's national culture if the Prime Minister of the country is an Irish or Scottish man or woman, this can bring about a political shift of doing things differently within the social systems, simply due to the leadership preference. National identity, is one's identity or sense of belonging to one state or to one_nation, this is the sense of a nation as a unified whole, as represented by distinctive traditions, culture, language, and politics. National identity can refer to the subjective feeling one shares with a group of people about a nation, regardless of one's legal citizenship status. Expression of one's national identity seen in a positive light is known as **patriotism**, which is, characterized by national pride and positive emotion of love for one's country.

The extreme expression of national identity is known as chauvinism, which refers to the firm belief in the country's superiority and extreme loyalty toward one's country. An example here could be what the Germany did to the Jewish people.

Research notes[40] that, a culture is influenced to a great, extent, by the agent or institution that disseminates information within that culture as well as the attitudes and influences on that agent. Since the beginning of the modern age, the dissemination of information has been carried out mainly by academics such as Wissenschaftler, the Church and the State in various combinations, source[41].

---

[40] (Münch 1990)
[41] http://www.interculture-journal.com/index.php/icj/article/viewFile/178/280

Looking at it from a leadership and political aspect, oftentimes countries within Africa usually tend to shape the national culture's identity according to the leader's culture and tribe; and politically. In the case of Uganda (case in point), research indicates that, Uganda's leadership excises a lot of nepotism within their cultural social systems within areas such as employment sector, tourism sector, land ownership, towards the sitting president's tribe. On the other hand, having said that, national culture encompasses other attributes such as language, food, music, etc., to name a few. Therefore, different subcultures could help in forming a national culture regardless of the nepotism in politics. For example, the main language of the country may not change because its leadership, rather another subordinate culture within the country such as Scottish music may contribute towards national culture and its identity. As alluded before by Münch 1990[42] and Wissenschaftler[43]; that in those times culture was greatly influenced by the institution that disseminates information within that culture and the beginning of the modern age, the dissemination of information was carried out mainly by academics. Subsequently it can be argued that, the national culture identity is for the most part fluid according to the times in certain aspects, in contemporary times one can allude that, the media has had greater influences in promoting and shaping aspects of a countries national identity by promoting items such as music, food, tourism , sports and so on.

Other researches note that, National identity can be most

---

[42] Ibid 40
[43] Ibid 41

noticeable when the nation confronts external or internal enemy, Guibernau, Montserrat (2004) and natural disasters. An example of this phenomenon is the rise in patriotism and national identity in the United States of America (USA) after the terrorist attacks on September 11, 2001. According to Ross[44], the identity of being an American are salient after the terrorist attacks and American national identity are evoked. Also Ashmore, Richard; Jussim, Lee; Wilder, David (2001), say that having a common threat or having a common goal unite people in a nation and adding Uko-Ima, Barrister (2014)[45], enhance national identity.

Sociologist Anthony Smith[46] argues that national identity has the feature of continuity that can transmit and persist through generations. By expressing the myths of having common descent and common destiny, people's sense of belonging to a nation is enhanced. However, national identities can disappear across time as more people live in foreign countries for a longer time, and can be challenged by supranational identities, which refers to identifying with a more inclusive, larger group that includes people from multiple nations.

Other researchers suggest that, as immigration increases, many countries face the challenges of constructing national identity and accommodating immigrants. Some countries are more inclusive in terms of encouraging immigrants to develop a sense of belonging to their host country. For example, Canada has the highest permanent immigration rates in the world. The

---

[45] Ibid 37
[46] Ibid 37

Canadian government encourages immigrants to build a sense of belonging to Canada and has fostered a more inclusive concept of national identity which includes both people born in Canada and immigrants. Some countries are less inclusive. For example, Russia has experienced two major waves of immigration influx, one in the 1990s, and the other one after 1998. Immigrants were perceived negatively by Russian population and were viewed as "unwelcome and abusive guests". Immigrants were considered outsiders and were excluded from sharing the national identity of belonging to Russia.

In some cases, national identity collides with a person's civil identity. For example, many Israeli Arabs associate themselves with the Arab or Palestinian nationality, while at the same time they are citizens of the state of Israel, which is in conflict with the Palestinian nationality. Taiwanese also face a conflict of national identity with civil identity as there have been movements advocating formal "Taiwan Independence" and renaming "Republic of China" to "Republic of Taiwan. Residents in Taiwan are issued national identification cards and passports under the country name "Republic of China", and a portion of them do not identify themselves with "Republic of China," but rather with "Republic of Taiwan".

Scholars note that, Identity is viewed in psychological terms as "an awareness of difference", a "feeling and recognition of 'we' and 'they'". Self-categorization National Identity requires the process of self-categorization and it involves both the identification of 'In-group' (identifying with one's nation), and differentiation of 'Out-groups' (other nations). By recognizing commonalities such as having common descent and common destiny, people identify with a nation and form an 'In-group', and at the same time they view people that identify with a different nation as 'Out-groups' noted in Smith, Anthony (1991)[47]. Social identity theory suggests a positive relationship between identification of a nation and derogation of other nations. By identifying with one's nation, people involve in intergroup comparisons, and tend to derogate 'Out-groups'. However, several studies including Hopkins, Nick (2001)[48] have investigated this relationship between national identity and derogating other countries, and found that identifying with national identity does not necessarily result in 'Out-group' derogation.

We must note, culture is learned and inherited; therefore, this is what gives the national culture's identity the ability to change according to the changing social systems and times.

Cultural appropriation and identity

It's been suggested by sociologist that Cultural appropriation is dealing with the adoption of the elements of one culture by members of another culture. Cultural appropriation, often framed as cultural misappropriation, is sometimes depicted as harmful and is claimed to be a defilement of the collective intellectual property rights of the originating culture. Often unavoidable when multiple cultures come together, cultural appropriation can include using other cultures' traditions, food, fashion, symbols, technology, language, and cultural songs. Critics, suggest that, cultural appropriation differs from

---

[47] Ibid 47
[48] Ibid 37

acculturation, assimilation, or cultural exchange in that the "appropriation" or "misappropriation" refers to the adoption/adaptation of these cultural elements in a colonial manner. In this context, elements are copied from a minority culture by members of a dominant culture, and these elements are used outside of their original cultural context sometimes even against the expressly stated wishes of members of the originating culture, source[49].

Cultural appropriation, one can see that is simply not a bad notion, if someone is simply celebrating the individuals' culture. This only becomes a problem when one takes that culture and claims ownership of that culture as their own. This could be seen as, identity theft, whereby, the dominant culture claims ownership of a culture that they did not create and use it to their advantage or privilege to benefit them. For example, hair styles such as dreadlocks, if a European wears braids or cornrows and a black person wears braids or cornrows and go for a job interview, it's been reported that if both of these individuals are given employment the black person would be told to cut their hair or style it a certain way, whilst the European person is given the privilege to wear the hair. Whilst the European person is celebrated wearing someone else's cultural hair style the person that comes from that culture of thought is told to straighten their hair or use a better style that is fitting for that job role. This becomes cultural appropriation in that the European person is now allowed to own the hair style whilst the individual whose culture it comes from has been told

---

[49] https://en.wikipedia.org/wiki/Cultural_appropriation

to remove the style or omit it.

This becomes a form of identity theft, whereby, the individual that originally owns the culture has been told to not wear it. This individual's cultural identity has been undermined at high regard whereby this can cause psychological issues of self-identity. Cultural appropriation, that is used as a tool of ownership instead of celebration creates a distortion of cultural identity; this can create cognitive dissonance[50] within the people of that culture that own the culture in which that cultural thought or creation stem from.

In a similar vein, researchers also note that, when people have a history that makes you a people of an esteem culture, if you remove the history of that esteemed people, that history disappears, and nobody will be lamenting the loss of that history, so owning the history or a cultural history is important where cultural appropriation is concerned. There are psychological links between what someone thinks of themselves, or what someone thinks of their people and their history, scholars in this regard, talk about personal esteem which means self-esteem then you have group esteem which is what you think of your group or what you think of your race, cultural esteem.

It's learned that self-esteem and cultural esteem is not the same thing, someone can have very high self-esteem and very low racial esteem, where they think very badly. For example of other black people meaning their racial or cultural group, it's

---

[50] Cognitive dissonance (the state of having inconsistent thoughts, beliefs, or attitudes especially as relating to behavioural decision and attitude change)

been suggested that most black people have very high self-esteem and very low racial esteem hence why black people are well known in disagreeing with each other and to conflict with each other. When someone thinks very low of their group or culture, cultural appropriation in this regard can be easily taken up and owned by another group from the original owners of that culture.

In this chapter, we've explored cultural identity touching on issues such as immigration and sub-cultures. We've learned that cultural identity depends upon the person who holds and maintains the values towards it, also can be dependent upon factors such as the family, environment, country, subordinate sub-cultures, and immigration. We have learned the subject of culture can also be fluid according to the current changing times and generations.

CHAPTER

41

FOUR

IDENTIFYING THE SELF

Identifying the self-varies according to the environment, the social networks, family, and self.

PSYCHOLOGICAL PERSPECTIVE

William James 1830s notes that, the self can be put in three elements, which entails the material, the social and spiritual. The material me includes not just the body, but also clothes, home, wealth, possessions and works; the social me, James saw this as about recognition one gets from others, people and he expresses that by nature are social and gregarious and it would be impossible to have a meaningful sense of one's self without the respect and concern of others. Expressing that the spiritual me is the collection of my states of consciousness, my psychic faculties and dispositions taken concretely; noted in Rogers (2003) Pg 231, source[i]. James documented that there are multiple social selves, whereby people show different sides of themselves to different people, different selves that they show to parents, their teachers, their friends, their customers to those who work for them. He suggested that a man's fame or honor were crucial parts of his social self, and important influences on his behavior whereas others, for example, may flee from a city infected with cholera a priest or doctor would consider this incompatible with his honor and stay, noted in Rogers (2003) Pg 231.

The above perspective asserts that, the value of identifying the self can be fluid when the self is identified within environmental surroundings. One can say this is a true notion but according to the individuals culture, as suggested before in Chapter One, in certain countries and cultures in Africa identifying the self can stay the same within different social environments across the board, whereby a king of a village for example has to identify one as a king regardless whether he is in his village, at a school, hospital and so forth. This decorum is enjoyed by all royals in the world but expression can vary according to cultural expressions of identity.

Then in this regard identifying the self-according to social, the spiritual, and the material can be classed as labels within categories. This is where the fluid individual is oftentimes limited to the labeled self. Having said that, the boxes that society or you put yourself in, can limit the self to progress oftentimes this is done unconsciously or due to upbringing or parental nurturance. In identifying the self, one must grow at different stages in life, in that, the age group process of identity varies on one's cognitive process and mental capacity. Let's say one was born with a physical disability, for the most part, their identity maybe heavily shaped by their parents or care givers. In this context, most of their life experiences are advocated by others, however, if the individual is supported to live independently and encouraged to explore the world and own their experiences then identifying the self begins to be shaped by the individual themselves.

The process in which identifying the self takes place becomes a journey that the individual takes, which as we explore seems to be carried by many different paths and turning. Research suggest that, this concept of identifying the self as an individual or as independent; heavily took place in the western countries as the age of reason started to grow and develop so was the self-identifying the self. In support, Smith and Bond, Pg 104[51], note that, the perception of oneself as an independent agent has been a major emphasis in the life of western industrial nations in recent times. More so that values such as freedom and self-determination are highly esteemed, and many members of these nations will, if asked, characterize themselves as possessing traits and abilities, such as intelligence, friendliness, modesty or what you will. Further explaining that, the word "individual" had a decidedly different meaning in the English language.

Williams[52] stresses, this word "individual" was used to refer to each of the members of the Trinity, God the Father, God the Son, and God the Holy Spirit. Further expressing that, the religious imagery that was predominant at the time an individual was not a separate entity, but was indissolubly linked to others, whose identity was collectively defined.

This suggests that, as time and reason progress one must define themselves according to the social systems that have been put in place within that cultural norms of the country. This is done whilst independently defining the self-according to the accepted norms of that cultural system of the country; or if the individual has an identity that is already self -consolidated which is not easily influenced by the boxes society has imprinted; defining the self becomes a self-responsible journey outside of those norms with an independent influence upheld by the self.

---

[51] Ibid 4

[52] James, William. The Principles of Psychology. New York: Dover Publications, 1890

In support, During Simon[53] note that "Individuals" don't have a single identity, they have identities, and they do so just because identities are based on partial traits (skin colour, socio-economic status, gender, nationality, region, profession, generation and so on). I am a man and a New Zealander, and an ectomorph, and bourgeois, and an academic, and Aquarian, etc. But not all identities carry equal weight, circumstances or have the same social consequences. Gender, race or ethnicity, and class are the identities, most of all, by which we are placed socially.

It can be said that when defining the self oftentimes some items such as culture may limit the self of defining the self independently. As noted before some cultures from within the African continent that practice inclusive social systems may limit the individual of defining the self independently, for example, cultural beliefs such as, marrying outside your culture or race being forbidden to name a few. In this context defining the self can be difficult according to cultural expectations whereby the individual feels a cultural obligation must be maintained regardless of what the self believes.

One is bound to wonder how does this affect the individual psychologically. Many cross-cultural psychologists have noted a difference between cultural construction of the self. Heine and Lehman express that cognitive dissonance arising from knowing that one has done something bad or foolish should be greater in cultures where an independent self is socialized. As noted in Smith and Bond [54], pg 109, in cultures socializing for interdependence, situational constraints and obligations largely

---

[53] Ibid 5
[54] Ibid 5

govern the behavior of individuals, and consequently, behavior is not typically seen as an accurate reflection of the individual's thoughts and attitude. Therefore, indicating that such cultures that are interdependent and that are inclusively inclined, can cognitively shape the selves defining of self via the obligations practiced within these cultures. In this regard, defining the self, without no cultural constrains, one must start unpacking some of the seasoned influences via cultural obligations to experience self-identifying the self and defining the self.

This is where self-awareness comes in. Self–awareness is being aware that we are objects of attention. Researches note that, self-aware individuals say that they reflect about themselves a lot, are always trying to go figure themselves out, are constantly examining their own motives, are alert to their own moods swings, and so on. Instead of focusing their attention outwards to other people or their surroundings they focus their attention inwards to themselves. As it were, Lord Pg 200[55] noted Self-aware individuals go through life scrutinising themselves in the mirror of their own imagination. In addition, it's been suggested that, when defining self, self-awareness is oftentimes the focus of the individual. Recommended rituals such as meditation are always marketed towards defining the self, yet some people seek other rituals such as religion. However, those that seek to use rituals such as religion will be looking outside the self to define the self.

On the other hand, Duval, Wicklund, and Wicklund[56] suggest

---

[55] Ibid 11

that, self-awareness exaggerates an individual's shortcomings. While Lord Pg 200, notes, everyone has at least some character flaws and everyone makes mistakes from time to time, but individuals differ in their re-actions to their own flaws and mistakes. People who pay little attention to themselves may remain blissfully unaware that they are making fools of themselves. People who frequently scrutinize their motives and feelings are less fortunate even if they are more realistic. May be when people are self-aware, they notice times when they do not live up to their own standards of acceptable behavior.

To quote Lord, Pg 189[57] research extensively, that;

"...people who lived in early European cultures did not have to worry about who they were; a person's self was defined and accepted by society from birth to death. In modern times, however, people have many choices about who they are and who they become. As a result, they may find it hard to a self-concept, to understand and fulfill their potential, and to relate to society. Modern people define themselves in part by constructing a self-schema or set of beliefs about how they typically deal with life events. The self-schema can be relatively simple or complex. It includes beliefs about people's past and possible future actions. It also includes beliefs about what people wish they were, what they think are obligated to be, what other people wish they would be, and what other people think they are obligated to be. People also define themselves by comparing themselves to others, we define our self – esteem and personal fulfillment by how well we are doing compared to others. Comparing ourselves upwards to others who are doing better can help plans improvement, but it can also

---

[57] Ibid 11

remind us of our shortcomings…"

RELATIONSHIPS IDENTITY

In this chapter will be discussing family relationships, boyfriend and girlfriend relationship, husband, and wife relationship and how they identify themselves and people within those relationships. It's been found that people identify themselves differently in relationships according to what relationship it is; family, man and woman relationships, husband and wife, business relationships and so forth.

The Cambridge dictionary, defines a relationship as the way in which two things are connected, source [58]. If this is accepted, then the question will be how we are connected to relate for example that between a boyfriend and girlfriend relationship, which can be connected in many ways. The connection could be sexual, attached, bloodline relation such as children, spiritual connection, or love. Husband and wife for the most part can be connected by the same attributes as the boyfriend and girlfriend, however they would have paper work and witness to seal the deal (oftentimes seen as a third party which is the government or the church). Family relationships connections, are often purely though bloodline, or via attachment though relations.

We have observed so far that for the most part relationships should be formed via different factors of connection. However, how relationships are identifying themselves varies according to

---

[58] http://dictionary.cambridge.org/dictionary/english/relationship:
definition of a relationship:

the connections formed. Therefore, what is important here is to form a relationship identity, in that, the connection of that relationship must help in giving that relationship an identity in some way or the other. One can assert that, if identity is fluid does it hold enough merit to identify our relationships? It can be said that some relationship identities can be changed, others such as family or bloodline relationships identities cannot be changed because these are biological relationship identities, whereby they are already identified and connected without the person's choice.

On the other hand, boyfriend, and girlfriend relationship identity may change forever and the connection may vary according to the new relationship identity. If say, the individuals conceive off springs they may obtain a new relationship identity of mother and father whereby bloodline connects them. However, if they did not intend to give birth to off springs during their relationship and one partner did not want the off spring to be birthed; the connection of their relationship and identity may change to a more contractual and bloodline relationship identity. In a similar vein, another boyfriend, girlfriend, or husband and wife relationship identity changing due to a seen or unseen contract relationship agreement. In this context it can be said that whenever there is a relationship there is a contract to adhere too, weather written or unwritten. For example, if one partner has children and the other doesn't, the partner that does not have any children would have picked a new identity of a step mum or dad. However, how they identify themselves within that relationship may vary according to their connection within the new identity that they have obtained within this relationship.

One can say that; some people may not have motherly or fatherly instincts due to either their upbringing or their learning and environmental experiences. For them therefore, to identify with this new role in their relationship may entail them learning new things to maintain the connection in the relationship, they would then, have obtained an identity that they were not ready for now.

Also, family relationship identities can also affect or contribute to how we identify ourselves in relationships. How we connect within our family relationships is critical for our identity, in that, if for example a child does not feel connected to his mother or father they would always seek that connection and identity somewhere else. If we take a case of a girl child, connecting with her father or a positive male figure, if connection is lost they would oftentimes seek this connection within their boyfriend or husband relationship whereby they seek to identify their partner within their relationship as fatherly figure. It could be though being needy emotionally, others are known to seek for this via being sexually promiscuous, this is also known as a common practice among Daddy less daughter. Whereby they are always seeking for that male comfort or company to validate them. On the other hand, other effects of fatherless daughters, individuals, can express this though self-mutilation. In a similar vein, fatherless sons, can also be affected by how they express and understand emotions or how to treat the opposite sex; usually the father's role in this regard is one who demonstrates to the son how to be a man or the role of the man within a relationship and society. Having explored the effects of fatherless sons and daughters, this can become overwhelming to the male or woman in this relationship.

The point here is what the fundamentals of a relationship are for one to identify with the relationship!! It's been said that the quality of your relationship largely decides the very quality of your life that you live. Relationships are formed on different levels to fulfill different types of needs, the needs maybe physical, psychological, social, financial, political, etc. Whatever the nature of the relationship whatever the type of relationship, still the fundamental aspect is you have a need to fulfill (no I have nothing to get I want to give). Giving is also as much a need as receiving something, therefore there is a need whatever kind of need, needs maybe diverse, accordingly relationships could be diverse. The moment we form a relationship, wanting to fulfill a certain need and if we do not fulfill that need and expectations then the relationship will sour because of failing to identify with that relationship.

How does this unfulfillment affect the individual psychologically? Oftentimes this depends on the need that was met to be fulfilling in the relationship, for example, if it was a psychological need, the individual could face issues of abandonment, fear of rejection in relationships. Therefore identifying herself or himself in relationships can become a struggle, especially if the individual has or is experiencing adult developmental trauma. In this context, the childhood traumas that he or she could have faced, such as sexual abuse, exposure to domestic violence, and traumatic loss or bereavement could be still lingering. In this regard, this could affect the individual forming a healthy relationship identity, within their relationships. It is not uncommon for people traumatized by key caregivers to end up with friendships, romantic relationships, and even work settings which are not positive for them. Research also reports that, they find people who fit their traumatic identity, even when they are trying to make different and better choices, their choices oftentimes can lead to re-traumatisation through repetition of the past.

The affected as highlighted above can be said that they usually, end up being around emotionally unavailable people, abusive or narcissistic people, or end up trying to rescue and fix people they date. They may also deliberately, want to find someone who can offer what they intellectually know they need and want, yet unconscious influences lead them down unwanted, unfamiliar paths. Frequently, there is a powerful "chemistry" with new relationships, which makes it seem like the relationship will be different, only to learn with disappointment that it is all too familiar. When friends try to warn them, it's not unusual for them to pick the new romance over a trusted friend. Repeatedly getting into destructive relationships can be disorienting and confusing, leading one to question one's self-understanding and locking one into the old identity, while preventing new identities from taking root. On the other hand, if it was a financial need within that relationship that was unfulfilled, the individual could fall into a deep psychological state of depression and seek other means of identifying themselves within that relationship. For example one may mask negativities in the relationship using substances such as alcohol to suppress the failed need to keep identifying themselves within that relationship whereby other needs can be met. In this regard, the substance use could cause emotional conflict within the relationship, and in turn this can if not maintained well, will dissolve the connection between the relationships. Scholars, and Professionals, when dealing with such events of identity loss, attachment loss, relationship loss, and traumas or psychological distress; have offered some scientific and alternative models, such as CBT (Cognitive behavioral therapy), Counseling, Mindfulness, Psycho-Pharmaceutical treatment, substance abuse recovery models and Meditation, to name a few. To help the individual, deal with their emotional or psychological journey towards recovery and self-worth/actualization.

PSYCHOLOGICAL PRESPECTIVE ON META- CUTURAL AWARENESS IN MARRIAGE HOW THEY CAN BE IDENTFIED FOR A HEALTHY CONNECT:

This discussion in this topical area is informed by researches which as extensively quoted below:

As noted by Ting, Toomey [59] researches that suggest:

> *"…marriage is an intense and continuous relationship that demands all our skills and commitment to sustain…"*

Fontaine further explains, that;

> *"…the potential for misunderstanding and conflict is enormous, not surprisingly, cross cultural marriages have higher divorce rates than arises because the whole range of cultural differences already discussed becomes relevant in this comprehensive relationship, engaging considerable conflict that, viable intercultural marriages provide a useful case study for intercultural relations generally, because the partners must have developed workable strategies for dealing with diversity and /or be receiving benefits that offset the greater losses. Fontaine maintains that, such couples create inter-cultural micro cultures that permit them to negotiate a shared life…"*

These micro cultures emphasize a focus on the ecological context of the tasks at hand, as one way of avoiding a power confrontation between my cultural way versus your cultural way. When differences do arise, partners often attribute their difficulties to a different cultural background rather than to the personality of their spouse.

---

[60] Ibid 59

This attributional style accords culture an external reality that becomes one feature of the task constraints to be considered and accommodated.

As noted in, Smith and Bond, Pg 287[60] , Fontaine indicates that;

"…what develops in time is an intercultural micro culture that has significant departures from either spouse's cultural heritage creative synthesis without a sense of cultural loss…"

Fontaine[61] analysis of intercultural marriages identifies two key components to their success, firstly, partners must be cognizant of their partners cultural heritage and secondly, they must accord that heritage legitimacy in their dealings with another both developments enhance the process of externalizing culture, also quoted in Smith and Bond[62];

"…People form relationships, to experience a certain sense of completeness with themselves. When they don't have that, they feel incomplete whatever the nature of the relationship. Although there is a basis to connect, as we have seen and explored, there is complex process of relationships and surrounding factors around them and building them. Identifying what they are, is also another process one must address. There are expectations, sadly, no human being can fulfill expectation as long as they are subjected to human error, especially if the expectations are unrealistic, and if the individual is unable to understand the source of the expectations. But if the individual was able to understand the source of expectations one could form a very beautiful relationship that can be identified beautifully.

---

[60] Reference *1998,*
[61] Ibid 4
[62] Ibid 4

> *It is inclusiveness that people seek to maintain a relationship, whether family, friendship relationships, husband and wife relationship, boyfriend, and girlfriend relationship…"*

ATTACHMENT

Similarly, for the most part, people are also socialized and identified by 'attachments'. In psychology both Ainsworth, and Bowlby sources[63] emphasize that 'attachment' is defined as a deep and enduring emotional bond that connects one person to another across time and space   It's been noted that, 'attachment' does not have to be reciprocal, one person may have an attachment to an individual which is not shared. Specific behaviors characterize attachment, towards different people, things, objects, and animals. For example, Bowlby[64], emphasizes that in children, such as seeking proximity with the attachment figure when upset or threatened.

It's found that lack of healthy attachments in relationships can affect identity and forming healthy relationships. Studies such as John Bowlby's[65] study of the forty-four juvenile thieves; it's reported that, in this study Bowlby takes a group of forty-four juvenile thieves with a control group of emotionally disturbed juveniles not guilty of any crime. They all attended child guidance clinics where Bowlby worked. Fourteen of the thieves showed many characteristics of affectionless psychopathy,

---

[63] https://simplypsychology.org/attachment.html psychological definition of attachment

[64] Ibid 64

[65] Ibid 64

compared with none in the control group. Of the two groups, about 43 per cent of the thieves had suffered complete and prolonged separation (six months or more) from their mothers, or established foster mothers, during their first five years of life. This compared with just 5 per cent of the control group. Twelve (83 per cent) of the affectionless thieves had experienced such separations, but only five (17 per cent) of non-affectionless thieves had done so. As noted in Gross et al Pg 57[66], Bowlby interpreted his findings in terms of maternal deprivation contributing to anti-social behavior was specifically linked to loss of the mother figure,. Therefore, this also indicates that loss of attachment within certain relationships such as family, can lead to affectionless and destructive behaviors, which can also affect healthy interactions within relationships and identity loss. With these findings, one can suggest that, relationship identities vary according to the relationship and its connection. It can therefore be said that, how one identifies themselves depends on which relationship it is and how they form an attachment towards that type of relationship, and is what will give the relationship the identity.

In this Chapter, we have explored that relationship identities entail the subject knowing the differences between attachment obligations and a connection, indicating that, to have a relationship does not mean you are relating, which implies that there should be a connection to relate to the subject. The question at hand is, what tools of connections the subject should seek for, to relate. In this regard, we can allude that, there is two types of connections which are, Blood Relational

---

[66] Ibid 2; References

connection and Spiritual Connection, this is what will justify the relationship identity that holds the relationship.

CHAPTER

59

FIVE

AUTHORS CORNER

Childhood/youth

I was born in Africa Uganda – a country popularized as '…The Pearl of Africa…' as baptized by the colonial Britain. This is where the source of River Nile, the longest river in Africa stems from. Uganda is also well-known for its beautiful wildlife and beautiful tropical parks, alongside the beautiful beaches with the bright sunsets along the shores of the largest lake in the center of Africa, namely Lake Victoria, not to mention other feeder and surrounding lakes. I spent a small part of my childhood in Uganda before I and my mother departed to the United Kingdom, it was there I started my primarily school education. To reminiscence, on my childhood spent in Africa the first five years of my life was amazing. As the last born on my mother's side, I remember being spoiled by my family. We had maids and maintenance people that looked after the house. I could play out a lot with other children. In the high-profile area we lived in everyone knew each other, now my African identity was being formed during this process. In the house we ate African food, mainly, and our main staple was Matooke, which is also the main national cultural food.

I remember my mum and my sisters would teach me cultural rituals such as kneeling to greet your elders. My sisters would take me to the national parks where I saw park animals such as birds of different colours, I would play with them whilst I ran on the green grass with huge trees. The air in Africa felt fresh and the sun would shine until late in the night. I remember, my elder sisters and brothers would speak to me in both English and Luganda the national language, I would hear my mum tell them off and demanding them to speak to me in our local language, at this point, unknowingly, my mum was shaping my cultural identity.

All throughout my childhood, my mum and family maintained that I understood and spoke my cultural language. They maintained that I ate my cultural food and understood the cultural customs and rituals. After I and my mother departed from Africa, I spent the rest of my childhood in the United Kingdom. I remember when I arrived in the United Kingdom the culture was different everything seemed to move so first whereas in Africa things moved slowly. I began to make new friends, started a new school, the culture was different I ate different foods more of English even though my mum maintained that we also ate African. However, for the most part I enjoyed my chicken and chips, MacDonald's, etc., alongside the cakes and the custards. I will not fib that I was not persuaded/influenced by the abundant variety/smell of food before me. Well the saying goes 'throw a fish into water and it will swim', and indeed I swam.

I spent most of my childhood trying to maintain two identities my African Identity at home and my newly and challenging identity. I recall at home in UK, not being allowed to speak in English because my mother wanted me to retain my cultural language. The contradiction being that if I spoke in English at home I would get beaten or punished; my mother alluded to me that I was able to speak in English outside her house but whilst in her house she expressed that she wanted me to only hold her cultural customs and practices. Mum expressed to me that this would help me maintain my true African identity as I would need it in the future if am to travel back to Africa. Well, I found this statement to be true, later captured by the adage '….East, West, home is the best…' Surprise, surprise, even President Obama went back to Africa to see and experience his African Kenyan heritage, despite highest achievements in the United States of America in particular and the accolades in the world in general.

During my childhood in the United Kingdom where I reside, my Mum ensured that she kept close with the people from the same culture as her. I remember we attended church a lot, they would worship in my mother's language, and I had friends of my age group from the same background in this church. There was a sense of belonging everywhere that every felt as we were all from the same African culture, and a sense of social identity and cultural identity, as unpacked in chapter, two and three of this book. Within the church, we would maintain celebrations of our cultural background, I often found that the social networks within the church were like a family, people often spent holidays and Xmasses together, and the pastor would hold gatherings at his house where we people would also bring our cultural food to eat together.

I was good friends with the pastor's children, we would hang out and go out places, and we also went to the same school at one point. I found that we kept closer together because we were from the same cultural background. At this point, it can be said that, there was a sense of lack of assimilation from amongst us with the other children in school as we had no shared cultural trust between us of which our parents formed within the church.

It was during my youth that I started making friends with people from the Afro-Caribbean culture, I found myself hanging around a lot of them and within their community. My youth was one full of experimenting, it was during this time I left my mother's house and was given my own accommodation at the age of 17years, and with it were accompanying and exhausting learning. I found that even without my mother I still retained most of the cultural customs that I had learned from her. Later in my youth I had to return to Africa, Uganda, with my mother for a visit. During this time in my life I felt a double consciousness that W.B. DU BOIS, spoke about in his book 'Souls of Black Folks' as mentioned in Chapter Three, the people in Africa saw me as an English girl they did not take me as an African girl. I asked why they expressed to me that my mannerism and how I reacted within certain situations were those of a European nature. Their reflection of me was that of a white English woman on the inside but just black on the outside, I found that my accent amused them and my dressing and my sense of self-pride made them wonder.

It was at this point that I started really questioning my identity, as shaped in the United Kingdom, where I was classed as an African woman and not European. This happens when I would tick boxes every time I would apply for a Job in the United Kingdom as an African. Yet in Africa itself the African people did not classify me as an African causing me ponder on this on my return to the United Kingdom (UK). I wondered why the British would see me as African even though I held a British Passport yet in converse, I felt not really accepted by both

Africa and Europe. This anomaly affected my spirit but I kept it locked inside me. Now, I never really spoke about it to my Mum , I remember, I would ask her questions about different things within her culture, all in the hopes that the more I knew the more Africa maybe would accept me.

It was later in my adulthood, I realised that my heritage regardless of where I lived, is what made me who I am and not the cultural customs or systems that are practiced. I learned that the cultural customs where systems that were used to maintain the attributes of that heritage. It was from then, I felt the understanding of my identity coming back to me and found myself fighting a lot with my identity. During my youth on one hand I would at times pull out the British card in certain areas due to my accent, on the other hand I would pull up the African card in certain functions due to my upbringing. As my African identity got shaped in my adulthood I began to embrace it more, irrespective of who felt I was African or not as I understood that citizenship had nothing to with my nationality or my birth right, as explained in Chapter One of this book.

Schooling/Education

How I have been schooled by my mother and family, I found was beneficial to my development as a person whereby it helps me keep a consistent mindset of knowing certain values, not just any value most importantly the African values and traditions. My mother gave me great knowledge about the importance of keeping inclusiveness when it comes to family whilst living in an exclusive society; schooled me to be aware of the importance of community by ensuring I attended church and traditional functions with her within her own cultural circles. I remember we would be taught to dance the African cultural dances and how to cook African food, how to wear the African dresses.

I started my Primarily School, where I experienced my childhood outside of my African tradition. The school was mixed but mostly white English children were the majority. I re-call when I started at the school, the children used to laugh at my quirky/fresh African accent before I acquired an English one. They would ask me questions about Africa and if African people lived with Lions. I would express myself with anger as I did not understand why they would think or ask such questions. Looking back at this now I realize that the media had a lot to do with how the picture of Africa was promoted, and me too was groomed with the same mindset, the more I resided in England. As I left Africa when I was quite young and could not remember much of the picture the media painted of a Africa, poor with hungry kids on the streets begging, roads that were made of soil and so forth. Until I went back to experience it myself, what I found and saw of a beautiful Africa that was not promoted by the media. My mindset changed.

The Africa I saw was the city of Kampala just like London City in Britain, of concrete roads, beautiful hotels, clubs, shops, building, etc. Similarly, the people were polite very sociable well-spoken and simple. On my return to England, I reflected on this.

As I continued with my primary school education, I started to adapt to the British culture and way of life. My secondary school education, I found made me an independent thinker. This, it appears was my persona as from quite a young age I refused to conform to any group during my high school days, and as always lead my own group in school. I was also a little troublesome, shall I say, a challenging young lady, at school seeking to identify herself and explore the world. To put it mildly, I was quite clever by half, but my curiosity about things and why they were the way they were. This put me in trouble with both my teachers and my mum. A notable pattern was that I would leave school early sometimes or not even come to school because I thought I was too good for school, my interest was in making money, having fun, and socializing with friends. Imagine!!

I used to make trouble in, or as they say, 'trouble maker at', school because of teasing about my African Identity by the white kids. I remember black and white kids used to have quite vicious snow and egg fights at school. After the secondary school, I started college, where I met this one teacher called Mr. Eric an amazing individual who taught me how to look at things from a different perspective. He ensured and indeed set aside that extra time out for me for my education. Now, he explained to me how it was not a bad thing being an individual who looked or thought differently from others. More so, taught me how to think outside the boxes of labels such as learning to create or embrace my identity.

After college, my university education was a wonderful experience and learning process for me, especially the subject of psychology. As I unpacked the Art of Psychology, it was now that I got to understand my whole process of my upbringing, culture, and my social networks, how they affected me, how they played a role on what and how I saw the world. Even though I went to church, religion had never provided, that kind of insight for me, and my spirit remained in flux about many things.

Gainsaid, higher education, provided me with the tools to seek and look deeper than what I was exposed. It was this deeper look-in about identity and how people presented themselves, hence the writing of this book today. Well I can say it here without any contradiction that for the most part people are like in a game of chess in this world, whereby they must play a role that they have been taught.

Identifying my self

Identifying myself therefore was not easy and still is in the process of self-actualization, as documented before in this book, that is, all the way from primary school I have been seeking for an identity to be comfortable in; it's now clearer that I was shaped by, and indeed share two cultures, namely, black African and white British. The process of identifying myself even within the journey of this book has enabled me to understand myself both socially, psychologically, physically, and spiritually. During my youth I veered away from my culture and people from my cultural background, by socializing more with people from the Afro-Caribbean background and other African cultures other than mine. This sharpened my cultural intelligence especially as I travelled abroad to other European countries where I experienced some common links amongst these people. The only point of reference, I saw and/or experienced was the felt-differences in social systems of these countries.

Whilst on this journey on youth development I let slip my

cultural identity yet very assertive with my personal identity. I found that within this process I carried my personal identity everywhere and within the people I socialized with. This made my social identity fluid, which enabled me to be receptive to other cultures that I socialized with. It was during my university days when I began to really explore my original/formative cultural identity in more depth, more so in all social aspect whilst retaining my culture at the same time. Am now able to engage and socialize without assimilating myself within the different cultures that I see or interact with during my travels. May be better put that, I have been able to adapt within the social environments.

Let me assert here that it is only when one can define oneself that one can really and authentically relate to every social environment. I now believe I have refined myself enough to identify myself in different environments without any contradictions. Therefore, my identity for the most part has been consolidated and authentically developed as I go, without being influenced by other norms or pressure. To refine myself I had to look more inwards rather than outside, this took a processing of meditation, reading, and researching about the things I learned during my travelling and along my travels.

I also found meditation to be helpful in re-defining myself. Meditation takes a process of being silent and listening to the self and the soul, I found time spent like this with the self once every evening and morning is the most useful and quality time that enables you to identify the real you and sets your vision for the day clear. My discipline for self-truth enabled me to go on journeys and meet people I never thought I would meet in my past, by this I have been able to give back to the universe by mentoring both young and old people with similar challenges. I have also been awarded and appreciated for this very work I do, by the community, organisations, and individuals. It's by this gift or blessing of knowing self and wanting to know and identify self that I have been able to do and carryout satisfying goals. As we exploring psychologist such as myself and others express that, the self-changes according to different environments, interactions, and relations to those environments.

Let me lastly repeat here, *ad nauseum*, during my journey of seeking for self, I found that what is not easily changed is character, regardless of what environment, interactions, or social networks. Most characters that are formed stay the same, unless altered by substances such as drugs or alcohol or the ego.

AUTHOR'S NOTE:

I was challenged to write this book because of what I saw and learned within my environment, my work, and community. As I reflected, I felt there was a lack of understanding, what identity was on a baseline level and on every level that related to a subject (individual/person/human being). On further reflection, it dawned on me that our social networks society alongside cultures and family has a big influence in dictating for the most part how one defines themselves as we learned via the research noted within this book. In my travels I then found the topic of race and class to be salient factors that contribute to the subject of identity across the globe. The impact on me from the proceeding narrative made me want to explore the subject of identity, by this I felt the world needed to know the impact that psychology, has had towards identity hence why I explored perspectives of different studies and research in psychology to unpack this notion. As noted elsewhere above, also my lived experiences with identity pushed me to explore and understand the subject alongside my psychological profession.

C: Namugabi

psychologicalthinktank360@gmail.com

REFERENCES

Bowlby. (1969) *Attachment. Attachment and loss: Vol. 1. Loss.* New York: Basic Books.

Ainsworth, M. D. S. (1973). The development of infant-mother attachment. In B. Cardwell & H. Ricciuti (Eds.), *Review of child development research* (Vol. 3, pp. 1-94) Chicago: University of Chicago Press.

W.E.B DU BOIS, THE SOULS OF BLACK FOLK 1903, Pg 2, in The Dover Thrift Edition edited 1994.

JOSEPHINE HENNESSY and MICHAEL A. WEST: SMALL GROUP RESEARCH, Vol. 30 No. 3, June 1999 361-382.

Intergroup Behavior in Organisations, A field Test of Social Identity Theory: Josephine Hennessy and Michael, A, West; First Published June 1, 1999

Wendy Rogers: Social Psychology, Experimental and Critical Approaches: Published 2003, Philadelphia.

Peter B. Smith and Michael H. Bond: Social Psychology Across Cultures. Second Edition, Published 1998.

Research Article:

Sociology exploring the architecture of everyday life: David, M, Newman et al 1958 published 1958

Lord, C, G, Published 1997, *Social Psychology*, Publisher Christopher P, Klein

The handbook of Identity, Theory, and Research: Seth J. Schwartz, Koen Luyckx, Vivian L. Vignoles, Published 2011

James, William. The Principles of Psychology. New York: Dover Publications, 1890.

Smith, Anthony (1991). National Identity. University of Nevada Press. pp. 8–15. ISBN 0874172047.

Hopkins, Nick (2001). "Commentary. National Identity: Pride and prejudice?". *British Journal of Social Psychology*

Guibernau, Montserrat (2004). "Anothony D. Smith on Nations and National Identity: a critical assessment". *Nations and Nationalism*. 10: 125–141. doi:10.1111/j.1354-5078.2004.00159.x. Archived from the original on 2015-11-23. Ross, Michael (Jul 4, 2005). "Poll: U.S. Patriotism Continues to Soar". *NBC News*. Archived from the original on 2015-11-17.

Ashmore, Richard; Jussim, Lee; Wilder, David (2001). *Social Identity, Intergroup Conflict, and Conflict Reduction*. USA: Oxford University Press. pp. 74–75. ISBN 0198031432.

Uko-Ima, Barrister (2014). *National Identity: Pragmatic Solutions for Democratic Governance in African Nations*. Xlibris LLC. p. 141. ISBN 9781499047950.

During, Simon (2005) 'Debating Identity', in Cultural Studies: a critical introduction. London: Routledge, pp. 145-152

Freud, S. (1961). The ego and the id. In J. Strachey (Ed.), The Standard Edition of the Complete Psychological Works of Sigmund Freud (Vol. 19, pp. 12-66) London: Hogarth Press. (Original work published 1923)

Sara Salih (2010) Representing Mixed Race in Jamaica and England from the Abolition Era to the present, 2010: Routledge research in Postcolonial literature.

Website references

https://simplypsychology.org/attachment.html

http://dictionary.cambridge.org/dictionary/english/relationship

Double consciousness-Wikipedia

https://simplypsychology.org/attachment.html

http://dictionary.cambridge.org/dictionary/english/relationship

Business dictionary

https://www.simplypsychology.org/Social-Facilitation.html

http://www.interculture-journal.com/index.php/icj/article/viewFile/178/280

https://en.wikipedia.org/wiki/Cultural_appropriation

http://www.bps.org.uk/system/files/Public%20files/Comms-media/Making%20better%20decisions.pdf

https://www.simplypsychology.org/Social-Facilitation.html

James, William. The Principles of Psychology. New York: Dover Publications, 1890

https://www.learning-theories.com/social-identity-theory-tajfel-turner.html

INDEX

AUTHOR'S PROFILE

Caroline Namugabi

 Profession Psychologist/McKenzie Friend at Law. A McKenzie Friend at Law represents people in courts, and advocates cases for low income people within the community.

Multiple Award winner in Leadership and Community work. Received a WAW honorary award and a Leadership BEFFTA Award, for her outstanding work of mentoring, Motivational, counseling, and youth work in the community.

Founder Uganda Youth Forum (UK) 2014-to date, brings all Ugandan youths together to deal with the issues at hand within their own community, this could be Identity issues, Social Justice issues, Legal issues and so on that the youths are dealing with.

Buganda Kingdom Deputy Youth Representative in the United Kingdom and Northern Irelands 2016-2019.

Founder of Think Tank 720 - 2017-to date, deals with bringing professions together as one people within the community and come up with solutions that will deal with the pending issues and information within the community.

Email: psychologicalthinktank360@gmail.com
ugandayouthforumuk@gmail.com

www.thinktank720.org.uk

www.ingramcontent.com/pod-product-compliance
Lightning Source LLC
Chambersburg PA
CBHW070029260726
48658CB00002B/556